Canine Culinar

www.canineculinarycreations.biz ©

"Gluten Free"

"Grain Free"

"Corn Free"

"Sugar Free"

Chef J.R. Davison

Author Chef J.R. Davison

ISBN-13: 978-0615665474 (DAV-JAX Publishing)

ISBN-10: 0615665470

Edited by Kimberly Smith Davison

™ Canine Culinary Creations "Grain-Free Edition"

davjaxpublishing@yahoo.com

*NOTICE:*
The information contained in this book is true and complete to the best of our knowledge. All the recipes in this cookbook have been carefully researched and tested on many dogs. However, you cannot rule out the possibility of other food allergies in certain breeds of dogs. The author nor the publisher cannot be liable in this case. The recipes are for special occasions, they are meant as a treat for your dogs regular diet and should not replace a proper balanced diet.

# www.canineculinarycreations.biz

# CHEF J.R. DAVISON

**Published By: DAV-JAX Publishing Company**

# Table of Contents

# *Acknowledgments*

This book is a compilation of knowledge and experience I've accumulated in more than 23 years as a professional chef. A full list of acknowledgments would stretch more pages than I could realistically devote. Many people have been helpful along the way and many names will go unmentioned – so I hope I'm forgiven.

A special thanks goes to my friend, mentor, and one of the best chefs that I know *Bruce Shamp*. Thank you for all your help on this version of the Canine Culinary Creations cookbook.

I would like to thank all my friends, and the visitors that came by my booths at all the events and shows that we attended. All the interest and support that everyone has given us and giving tons of suggestions to the kind of foods they would like in the next cookbook that I put out. I would also like to thank my beautiful wife *Kimberly Smith Davison* for believing in me and giving me support on the cookbooks and the support at all the shows and events. She was always by my side from morning 'till night, talking to all the visitors and selling all of the products that I had available.  I love you Kimberly, thank you.

# *Dedications*

*This book is dedicated to my family, my beautiful wife Kimberly Smith Davison, and to my four wonderful kids Russ, Justin, Tyler and Blake Davison.  I would also like to dedicate this to the one who inspired me to create this cookbook and is also my canine best friend, Jaxy.*

*I love you all*

# *Toxic Plants and Foods*

Please be aware that many types of household foods and plants from the yard, gardens and flowers can be very toxic to your dog. Pet owners need to be educated so they can protect their dogs from harm. On the next page, you'll find a list of the most common types of toxic foods, plants, and flowers. Please note that this is not a complete list, only those found in most households. There is more information on toxicities throughout the book. Contact your local veterinarian if you think your pet has ingested something harmful. Also, you can look up additional toxic foods and plants on the internet or call the poison control hotline.

Alcohol
Almonds
Amaryllis bulb
Apricot
Apple seeds
Autumn crocus
Avocado (leaves, seeds, stem, skin)
Azalea (entire Rhododendron family)
Begonia
Bird of Paradise
Bittersweet
Bleeding heart
Boxwood
Bracken fern
Buckeye
Buttercup
Caffeine
Caladium
Calla lily
Castor bean (can be fatal if chewed)
Cherries
Cherry seeds
Chinese sacred or heavenly Bamboo
Chocolate
Choke cherry (unripe berries)
Chrysanthemum
Clematis
Crocus bulb
Cyclamen bulb
Daffodil
Delphiniums
Dumb cane
Elderberry (unripe berries)
English ivy
Fig

Four-o'clock's
Foxglove
Garlic
Grapes
Hyacinth bulbs
Hydrangea
Holly berries
Iris corms
Jack-in-the-pulpit
Jim-son weed
Kalanchoe
Lantana
Larkspur
Lily
Lily-of-the-valley
Lupine
Macadamia nuts
Marijuana or hemp
Milkweed
Mistletoe berries
Monkshood
Morning glory
Mountain laurel
Mushrooms
Narcissus
Oak
Oleander
Onions
Peach seeds
Pencil cactus plant
Philodendron
Poinsettia
Potato (leaves and stem)
Raisins
Rhubarb leaves
Rosary Pea
Scheffelera
Shamrock
Tomatoes (leaves and stem)
Umbrella Plant

# *Poisonous Food*

Many pet owners believe that what is good for them is good for their canine best friend, too. Owners have to be very careful of the food that is put in front of the dog, as it could turn out to be poisonous.

One of the most common mistakes made by people is to give their pets chocolate and/or cocoa. Theobromine in chocolate is a diuretic and a cardiac stimulant. If ingested in large amounts, the dog becomes hyperactive and passes large volumes of urine. Vomiting can also occur. The heart rate accelerates and death is possible if the dog becomes very active. All types of cocoa, as well as cooking chocolate, are poisonous for dogs. Milk chocolate has less Theobromine, but is still harmful. The age of the dog, its size and energy level can determine how detrimental the ingestion can be to your dog.

Onions and garlic are other poisonous foods for dogs. Onions are especially toxic. Onions cause Emolytic anemia; that is, the red blood cells burst as they circulate through the body. Eating onions can cause diarrhea and vomiting. Passing dark colored urine, weakness, confusion, dizziness and accelerated heart rate are other symptoms of onion poisoning.

Left over pizza and some manufactured baby foods that contain onions and garlic can be poisonous for dogs. Mushrooms are also poisonous for dogs. Vomiting, diarrhea, convulsion, abdominal pain, liver or kidney damage, coma or death can all occur if mushrooms are eaten. Macadamia nuts are another poisonous food for dogs. These may cause muscle tremors, weakness and ultimately paralysis.

The seeds of fruits like apples, cherries and peaches contain cyanide and are poisonous for dogs. Smaller breeds are more likely to become very sick if they eat these seeds. Additional foods include tomato plants and stems. Tremors and heart arrhythmia are the direct results of eating tomato plants and stems. Grapes and raisins are also poisonous if ingested. Diarrhea, abdominal pain, vomiting and kidney failure can be results of dogs eating grapes and raisins. If your dog has eaten grapes or raisins, call your veterinarian immediately.

Caffeinated beverages are potentially harmful. A common mistake a human can make is to give their dogs sodas or other caffeinated drinks. Dogs should also never be given alcoholic beverages.

Feeding scraps to dogs during dinnertime should be avoided because most human food is potentially poisonous and can upset their stomachs. Owners should be careful and not let their dogs accidentally get into candy, leftovers or unattended foods. Many times the effects of poisoning are sudden and may be fatal. Prevention is always better than the cure and it can save you from regret and emotional distress. Keeping your dog away from poisonous food is the owners responsibility. The owner must discipline and urge their pets to eat only what is given in their bowls and plates. Always be attentive to your dog's behavior.

Some dog owners think their pets are the garbage disposal. Feeding your dog leftovers because you don't want to waste "good" food is potentially a health risk. Some leftover foods could be moldy or spoiled. Molds and bacteria go hand in hand. If your dog is a small breed, they may not be able to fight off infections caused by these bacteria. Indigestion, diarrhea and vomiting can occur. Chronic diarrhea can indicate secondary infections, if untreated, these infections can cause death. Foods are not the only dangerous items around the house. Dogs can sometimes eat medicines, rat poison and other chemical substances that are very toxic. Never give your pet medicines intended for human use. Medicines we take have different reactions for animals. Contact your veterinarian if your pet has ingested anything that could possibly be harmful or if you are unsure. Its better to be on the safe side.

# *Avoid Raw Foods*

Some dog owners think that raw meat and eggs are more "natural" and a great addition to a dog's diet. Raw meat, poultry, and eggs may contain bacteria such as salmonella that can make your dog very sick. Always serve cooked eggs, meats and poultry. Make sure discarded raw meats are not accessible to your dog to prevent accidental ingestion. Some people are misled in thinking adding a raw egg to a dog's food will give his coat a healthy shine. This myth is not true and is potentially harmful to your dog. In some parts of the country, fish found on the beaches can have parasites and are potentially fatal. Salmonella or other bacterial poisoning in dogs can have the same symptoms as in humans. Those symptoms can include loss of appetite, weight loss, lack of energy, fever, vomiting, and diarrhea. If your dog has any of these symptoms, contact your veterinarian immediately. Salmonella can be transmitted from dogs to people, so if you think your dog may be infected, wash your hands carefully after handling him or anything he uses, such as food dishes or toys. Not only is raw meat hazardous, bones in the meat can do damage. Bones can splinter when chewed, and if swallowed can tear the internal organs of your dog. Inspect any meats given to your dog and make sure there are no small bones.

# *Nutrition and Energy*

The human diet consists of natural foods that can also exist in dog food. Besides natural ingredients that humans consume on a regular basis, and that are easily available, there are natural foods not normally considered to be human foods. Examples

are horse meat, hog livers, and bone meal.
An all around balanced diet is important for
the health and longevity of your pet. A
dog's diet should consist of protein,
carbohydrates, fats, vitamins, minerals and
water. Meat is the most important part of
your dog's meal and it is also the most
common source of protein. There are other
great sources of proteins besides meat.
Eggs, milk and plant proteins also make up a
large group of protein rich sources easily
available.

Homemade dog foods contain nutrients that
are great energy sources. Some natural
foods supply more energy than others and
are used as energy sources, but these foods
can contain the largest quantities of fats and
carbohydrates. Fats are the primary source
of energy in any diet for a dog. Most
chopped and ground varieties of meat
contain fat. Fats also can be found in
vegetable oils or lard that are sometimes an
additive.

Carbohydrates are not as high of an energy
source as fats, but can be lower in cost.
Carbohydrates are useful to dilute the
protein in high-meat diets or lower the

caloric density of diets containing too much fat.

The most universally useful source of energy for dogs is corn oil. Corn oil supplies 250 calories in every ounce. When used as only fat in a food it also furnishes about ten times the amount of essential fatty acids needed by a dog. Corn oil is usually inexpensive, easily available and has a longer shelf life. Other oils that are an energy source for a dog are olive oil, peanut oil, safflower oil and soybean oil.

Growing puppies need food full of calories and nutrients, but once they become adult dogs this same diet can cause them to gain too much weight. If you are giving your dog food from a bag or a can, make sure to read the labels to determine if the food is age appropriate. It is important that your dog receives the proper amount of proteins, fat and carbohydrates according to age.

Dogs love yogurt, and it's good for them, too. If your dog is on an antibiotic, give him plain, unflavored yogurt to repopulate his digestive system with healthy bacterial flora. (Make sure the yogurt contains an active culture). If your dog has gas, adding a small amount of plain yogurt to the food can cut down on his distress.

Studies show both homemade food and dry food can be a nutritious and balanced diet for your dog. However, there are advantages and disadvantages for both. As long as the homemade food meets your dog's nutritional needs, you just need to balance the benefits and potential problems with your dog's age, health, preferences and your budget. Then decide which works best. A combination of both may be the best choice.

# *Advantages of Homemade Dog Food*

One of the greatest advantages of homemade dog food is that you can add in any nutritional ingredients without your dog knowing it. Homemade dog food lets the owner decide what is going into their pet's meal. The owner knows what chemicals are present and the quality of the food. Good homemade dog food can also be a nice change to the daily routine. Some homemade dog food is high in fiber and helps to keep the intestines healthy. Avoiding sugary and over processed dog foods, and giving your dog homemade food, will ensure the health of your pet.

Most manufactured dog foods can provide adequate levels of nutrition for your dog, but not optimum levels. Your dog can be ingesting large amounts of harmful chemicals if he is only consuming manufactured foods. As homemade food is better for humans, it can be the same for dogs. The fun of making your own food is being able to create the shapes, color, size, and texture of the food. Your dog can have something different and not get bored. This is great for finicky eaters. Homemade dog food will be fresh and you can have greater piece of mind knowing it doesn't contain poisonous or harmful ingredients. Please be aware of your pet's food allergies before preparing any of these recipes. Be sure to pay close attention to the ingredients in each recipe. Make sure the recipe doesn't contain ingredients that your dog is allergic to or doesn't like.

# Doggy Entree

# *Lamb & Rice*

- ✔ 1 pound ground lamb (beef if you wish)

- ✔ 1/2 cups un-cooked brown rice

- ✔ 2 stalks cut broccoli

- ✔ 3 medium potatoes (cubed)

- ✔ 3 medium carrots (cubed)

- ✔ 1/2 cup fresh chopped parsley

- ✔ 5 cups water

Brown ground lamb in a frying pan. Boil 1 gallon of water, add approximately 4-5 cups of water into a crock pot. Add cubed potatoes to the frying pan. Add remaining ingredients to the crock pot and add enough hot water to cover. Mix in 1/2 cup brown rice. Cook until rice is soft. Allow to cool completely and serve as desired. Store in refrigerator.

# *Beef & Rice*

- ✔ 16 quarts stew pot with enough olive oil to coat bottom of pot

- ✔ 5 pounds ground beef

- ✔ 2 large cans chicken broth

- ✔ 4 cups water

- ✔ 3 pound bag frozen peas

- ✔ 3 pound bag brown rice

- ✔ 1 teaspoon fresh chopped parsley

Brown ground beef in olive oil. Add broth, water and peas to cooked beef. Bring to a boil. Add brown rice and parsley, stir well, cover and bring to a boil again. Reduce heat to low and simmer covered for 1 hour. Allow to cool completely and serve as desired. Store in refrigerator.

# *Minced Meat & Rice*

- ✔ 1 pound low grade mince meat

- ✔ 1 pound frozen mixed vegetables (no onions or mushrooms)

- ✔ 2 cups rice

- ✔ water (to cover ingredients)

- ✔ 3 cups beef broth

- ✔ 1/2 cup fresh chopped parsley

Chop up minced meat into a large saucepan, cover with water and bring to boil. Add vegetables, rice and add beef broth to cover and parsley. Simmer until rice is soft, adding more water if necessary. Allow to cool completely and serve as desired. Store in refrigerator.

# *Yummy Meat Stew*

- ✔ 1 cup ground meat (turkey, lamb or hamburger)

- ✔ 1/2 cup cooked rice

- ✔ 1/4 cup potato (cubed)

- ✔ 1/2 carrot

- ✔ 1 cup water

- ✔ 1/2 cup frozen peas

Cut meat into small pieces, add cubed potatoes and sliced carrots. Add all ingredients into stock pot; add 1/2 cup water. Bring to a boil. Check stew and add water if necessary. Add rice to stew, stir and keep boiling for 15 minutes. Remove from heat. Strain the juice into a separate pot. Allow to cool completely. Serve with juice to moisten. Store in refrigerator.

# *Mint Rice & Hamburger*

- ✔ 5 cups un-cooked brown rice

- ✔ 10 cups of water

- ✔ 2 pounds hamburger

- ✔ 1/4 cup dried mint

- ✔ 1/2 cup chopped fresh parsley

Add water and rice to stock pot and bring to a boil. Add cooked hamburger, mint and parsley. Mix until well blended. Continue boiling for 3 minutes. Reduce heat to low and simmer until all water is absorbed. Allow to cool completely and serve as desired. Store in refrigerator.

# Doggy Bag Stroganoff

✔ 1 pound leftover dog safe meat (make sure its gluten free)

✔ 3 tablespoons rice flour

✔ 1 cup frozen peas

✔ 1 cup frozen carrots

✔ 3 cups beef stock

✔ 1 cup gluten free sour cream

✔ 4 cups cooked gluten free pasta

✔ water

Add first 5 ingredients to crock pot. Add water to cover if necessary. Cook for 15 minutes on high. After vegetables are tender, add sour cream and cooked noodles. Cook for additional 30 minutes on low. Allow to cool completely and serve as desired. Store in refrigerator.

# *Growlin' Goulash*

- ✔ 1 pound cooked ground meat (beef, turkey, pork or lamb)

- ✔ 1/2 pound chicken livers and gizzards, (chopped)

- ✔ 2 hard boiled eggs cooked and chopped "include the ground-up egg shells" (shells are high in protein)

- ✔ 2 cups cooked brown rice

- ✔ 3 cups combined fresh vegetables (broccoli, sweet potatoes, green beans, carrots, peas) (no onions or mushrooms)

- ✔ 1 can of mackerel oil (do not drain)

Blend all vegetables in processor. Mix all ingredients in large stock pot. Add enough water to cover and mix well. Cover the pot and simmer for approximately 2 hours, stirring occasionally. Allow to cool completely and serve as desired. Store in refrigerator.

# *Fetchin' Feast*

✔ 1 pound cooked, ground meat (chicken, beef, liver, turkey)

✔ 1 package of frozen mixed vegetables (no onions or mushrooms)

✔ 1 cup of cooked spinach

✔ 4 cups cooked rice

✔ 1/3 cup quinoa

✔ 1 teaspoon grated ginger

✔ 2 tablespoons tomato paste

✔ 1 teaspoon fresh ground parsley

Mix all ingredients except rice into large stock pot and add enough water to cover. Cook 20 minutes on medium, stirring occasionally. Add cooked rice and mix until well blended. Allow to cool completely and serve as desired. Store in refrigerator.

# *Come-N-Get It Casserole*

✔ 1 pound cooked, ground meat (beef, finely chopped lamb, chicken, turkey)

✔ 1/2 cup sliced green beans

✔ 1 carrot finely shredded

✔ 1 package flavored gravy mix (DRY)

✔ 1 small potato finely shredded

✔ 1 stick celery finely diced (remove the strings)

✔ 1 package gluten free crackers (crumb in food processor)

✔ 2 cups water

Add all ingredients into a large bowl and mix until well blended. Pour into greased casserole dish and bake at 350F for 45 minutes. Remove and place ground up crackers on top of casserole and bake until crackers are golden brown. Allow to cool completely and serve as desired. Store in refrigerator.

# *Paw-Fect Casserole*

- ✔ 1 cup beef or chicken broth

- ✔ 1 zucchini squash, chopped

- ✔ 1 yellow squash, chopped

- ✔ 2 carrots, shredded

- ✔ 1 pound stew beef (pre-cooked)

- ✔ 1 package gluten free crackers (crumb in food processor)

Mix all ingredients, except crackers, in large bowl and mix well. Pour into greased casserole dish and bake at 350F for 35 minutes. Remove and place crackers on top of casserole and bake until crackers are golden brown. Allow to cool completely and serve as desired. Store in refrigerator.

# *Rompin' Risotto*

✔ 2 tablespoons olive oil

✔ 1 potato, peeled and finely chopped

✔ 2 ounces cooked white rice

✔ 3 ounces cooked chicken, chunks

✔ 2 tablespoons plain gluten free yogurt

✔ 1/2 teaspoon chopped parsley

Heat the olive oil in saute pan then add the potato pieces and saute until tender. Stir while adding the rice. Mix in the chicken and reduce heat to low. Continue stirring for an additional 2-3 minutes. Stir in the yogurt and reduce the heat to simmer. Cover and simmer for 5 minutes, stirring occasionally. Allow to cool completely and serve as desired. Store in refrigerator.

# *Down Home Doggy Meal*

- ✔ 1 pound of ground beef or chicken

- ✔ 1/3 cup olive oil

- ✔ 6 cups water

- ✔ 3 cups frozen mixed vegetables (no onions or mushrooms)

- ✔ 1 small can kidney beans

- ✔ 1 1/2 cup cooked white rice

Brown meat in large stock pot, then add olive oil. Cook for 5-7 minutes then add water. Bring to boil, and then add vegetable mix and kidney beans and cook for additional 15 minutes or until vegetables are tender. Add rice and mix well. Reduce heat to low and simmer for 5 minutes, stirring frequently to avoid sticking. Allow to cool completely and serve as desired. Store in refrigerator.

# *Pawsta*

- ✔ 1/2 pound gluten free pasta

- ✔ 3 boneless, skinless chicken breasts

- ✔ 1/2 pound brown rice

- ✔ 6 ounces beef or chicken liver

- ✔ 2 cups water

- ✔ 1/2 pound frozen mixed vegetables (no onions or mushrooms)

- ✔ 8 ounces non-fat, gluten free cottage cheese

- ✔ dry Italian seasoning (to taste)

# (Continued Pawsta)

Place liver and rice in large stock pot, add water. Bring to a boil. Turn down heat and cook for 20 minutes. Season chicken with dry Italian seasonings and bake in oven at 350F for 30-45 minutes, or until a little crispy. After the chicken is done, boil 1 gallon of water in a large stock pot, add pasta. Cook 8-10 Minutes. Mix rice, vegetables, chicken and liver. Mix into a separate large bowl. Add pasta and cottage cheese, stir well. Serve mixed with your dog's favorite dry dog food.

# *Doggy Meat Loaf*

- ✔ 1 pound ground beef

- ✔ 8 eggs

- ✔ 1 cup cooked white rice

- ✔ 1/2 cup gluten free cracker crumbs

By hand, in a large mixing bowl, blend all items together until well blended. Pour into an oblong cake pan sprayed with pan spray. Bake at 350F for 35-45 minutes. Allow to cool. Carefully invert on to plate and frost with sour cream or instant mashed potatoes. Allow to cool completely and serve as desired. Store in refrigerator.

# *Dawg-on Meatballs*

✔ 1 1/2 pounds ground hamburger

✔ 3 1/2 cups cooked white rice

✔ 3 eggs

Mix all ingredients together in a bowl, form into meatballs. Brown meat balls in frying pan or bake at 350F for 10-15 minutes. Allow to cool completely and serve as desired. Store in refrigerator.

# *Leash Quiche*

- ✔ 6 eggs

- ✔ 1 cup skim milk

- ✔ 1/2 cup chopped bacon

- ✔ 1 1/2 cups shredded cheddar cheese

- ✔ 9 inch gluten free pie shell

- ✔ 2 tablespoons fresh parsley

Mix all ingredients together then pour into pie shell. Bake at 375F for 35-45 minutes. Allow to cool completely and serve as desired. Store in refrigerator.

# *Chicken Critters*

- ✔ 3 boneless, skinless chicken breasts
- ✔ 1 cup cooked white rice
- ✔ 1 cup cooked 1 inch sliced carrots
- ✔ 1 cup low-fat, gluten free cottage cheese

Boil chicken breasts in a small amount of water until done; chop. Cook carrots until tender. In separate large bowl, mix the chicken, carrots, rice and the cottage cheese. Can add broth from the chicken if it seems too dry, allow to cool completely and serve as desired. Store in refrigerator.

# *Hot Diggity Dog*

✔ 1 hot dog (low fat, low sodium)

✔ 1 slice cheese

Cut hotdog into 1 inch pieces. Spread out on a microwave safe plate. Put pieces of cheese on top. Microwave until the cheese is runny. Allow to cool completely and serve as desired. Store in refrigerator.

# *Jerky Dogs*

✔ 1 pound low fat hot dogs

Slice hot dogs into thin lengths.  Place on 3 layers of paper towel on a microwave safe plate.  Microwave on high for 5 minutes.  Remove from microwave let stand for 5 minutes.  Return to microwave and cook for a another 5 minutes then remove.  The hot dogs should be cooked until they are a jerky consistency.  Allow to cool completely and serve as desired.   Store in refrigerator.

# Doggy Treats

# *Drippin' Drop Biscuits*

- ✔ 2 1/2 cups buckwheat flour

- ✔ 1/2 cup nonfat powdered milk

- ✔ 1/2 teaspoon salt

- ✔ 1 teaspoon Splenda brown sugar

- ✔ 6 tablespoons meat drippings or margarine

- ✔ 1 egg, beaten

- ✔ 1/2 cup ice water

Lightly oil a cookie sheet. Combine rice flour, powdered milk, salt, and Splenda. Fold in meat drippings until mixture resembles corn meal. Mix in egg. Add enough ice water so that mixture forms a ball. Pat out dough to 1/2 inch thick. Cut into your dogs favorite shapes and bake at 350F for 25-30 minutes. Allow to cool completely and dry out until hard.

# *Sweat Potato Flour Biscuits*

- ✔ 2 cups buckwheat flour

- ✔ 1 1/2 cups sweet potato flour

- ✔ 2 cup rice puffs

- ✔ 1/2 cup nonfat powdered milk

- ✔ 1/2 cup hot water (add more if needed)

- ✔ 2 beef or chicken bouillon cubes

- ✔ 1/2 cup meat drippings

- ✔ 1 cup cold water

Dissolve bouillon cubes in hot water. Add cold water and drippings and mix well. In a separate bowl, mix both flours and rice puffs. Pour liquid ingredients into dry ingredients and mix well. Pat out dough to 1/4 inch and cut into your dog's favorite shapes. Place on an un-greased cookie sheet and bake at 300F for 1 hour. Allow to cool completely and dry out until hard.

# *Quinoa Biscuits*

- ✔ 8 cups  buckwheat flour

- ✔ 1 cup quinoa

- ✔ 1 1/2 cups nonfat powdered milk

- ✔ 3 cups chicken broth

- ✔ soy milk for glaze

Mix flour, quinoa, and powdered milk.  Add 2 cups broth; mix well with hands until dough gets stiff.  Add more broth as necessary.  Roll dough to 1/4 inch thick. Cut biscuits into your dog's favorite shapes. Place on un-greased baking sheet.  Brush each lightly with soy milk. Bake at 300F for 45 minutes.  Allow to cool completely and dry out until hard.

# *Yeast Biscuits*

- ✔ 1 package dry yeast
- ✔ 1/2 cup warm water
- ✔ 6 cups buckwheat flour
- ✔ 2 cups beef broth (warm)
- ✔ 1 cup flax seed meal
- ✔ 1/2 cup nonfat powdered milk
- ✔ 1 cup flax seed
- ✔ 1/4 cup margarine or butter
- ✔ 2 cups ground fiber cereal
- ✔ 1/4 cup honey
- ✔ 1 egg, beaten

# (Continued Yeast Biscuits)

In small bowl, dissolve yeast in warm water. In large bowl combine broth, powdered milk, margarine, honey, egg. Add yeast/water and mix well. Stir in flour, flax seed meal, flax seed and ground fiber cereal. Mix well. Knead flour by hand and continue kneading for 4-5 minutes until dough is not sticky.

Pat out dough to 1/2 inch thickness and cut into your dog's favorite shapes. Place on a greased cookie sheet, cover lightly and let set for 20 minutes. Bake at 350F for 45 minutes. Allow to cool completely and dry out until hard.

# *Cheese & Rice Puff Biscuits*

- ✔ 2 cups rice puffs

- ✔ 1/4 cup butter or bacon drippings

- ✔ 1 egg, beaten

- ✔ 1 1/2 cups hot water

- ✔ 1 cup flax seed meal

- ✔ 1/2 cup nonfat powdered milk

- ✔ 1 cup flax seed

- ✔ 4 oz (1 cup) grated cheese

- ✔ 3 cups buckwheat flour

## (continue Cheese & Rice Puff Biscuits)

In large bowl put rice puffs, butter/bacon drippings; let stand for 5 minutes. Stir in powdered milk, grated cheese, and egg. Add flax seed meal and flax seed. Add 1 1/2 cups hot water and mix well. Add flour, 1/3 cup at a time, mixing well after each addition. Knead 3-4 minutes, adding more flour if necessary to make very stiff dough. Pat or roll dough to 1/2 inch thickness. Cut into your dog's favorite shapes. And place on a greased baking sheet. Bake at 300F for 45 minutes. Allow to cool completely and dry out until hard.

# *Cheese-N-Bacon Biscuits*

- ✔ 1 cup buckwheat flour

- ✔ 1 cup grated cheddar cheese

- ✔ 1/2 cup chopped crispy cooked bacon

- ✔ 1 tablespoon soft butter or margarine

- ✔ 1/2 cup  soy milk

Mix flour and cheese together.  Add bacon and softened butter.  Slowly add milk until dough is stiff.  Knead on floured surface to make a very stiff dough.  Roll out to 1/4 inch thickness.  Cut into your dog's favorite shapes and place on an un-greased cookie sheet.  Bake at 350F for 25 minutes.  Allow to cool completely and dry out until hard.

# *Veggie Biscuits*

- ✔ 1 cup buckwheat flour

- ✔ 1/2 cup grated cheese

- ✔ 1/2 cup cooked peas or carrots

- ✔ 1/4 pound margarine

- ✔ 2 cups nonfat powdered milk

- ✔ 2 cups water

Mix all ingredients together in a large bowl. Add enough water to help form into a ball. Chill 1 hour, roll onto floured surface and cut into your dog's favorite shapes. Bake at 375F for 15 minutes or until biscuits are slightly brown. Allow to cool completely and dry out until hard.

# *Beef Biscuits*

- ✔ 2 1/2 cups buckwheat flour

- ✔ 1/2 cup nonfat powdered milk

- ✔ 1 teaspoon Splenda

- ✔ 1 teaspoon salt

- ✔ 1 egg

- ✔ 1 teaspoon beef or chicken bouillon cubes

- ✔ 1/2 cup hot water

In a large bowl, dissolve bouillon in hot water. Cool to room temperature. Add remaining ingredients. Knead for 3 minutes and form dough into a ball. Roll onto a floured surface 1/2 inch thick and cut into your dog's favorite shapes. Place on a greased baking sheet. Bake at 325F for 30 minutes. Allow to cool completely and dry out until hard.

# *Bacon Biscuits*

- ✔ 5 cups buckwheat flour

- ✔ 1/2 cup nonfat powdered milk

- ✔ 2 eggs

- ✔ 10 tablespoons vegetable oil or bacon fat

- ✔ 1 teaspoon salt

- ✔ 1 1/3 cup cold water

Mix all ingredients until well blended. Roll pieces of dough into 2 inch balls. Place on a greased cookie sheet. Bake at 350F for 35-40 minutes. Allow to cool completely and dry out until hard.

# *Glazed Dog Biscuits*

- ✔ 1 envelope dry yeast

- ✔ 1/4 cup warm water

- ✔ 1/2 cups Splenda

- ✔ 5 cups buckwheat flour

- ✔ 2 cups fiber cereal

- ✔ 1 cup sorghum flour

- ✔ 1/2 cup nonfat powdered milk

- ✔ 4 cups beef or chicken broth

### "Glaze for Biscuit"

- ✔ 1 large egg

- ✔ 2 tablespoons soy milk

## (Continued Glazed Dog Biscuits)

Sprinkle the dry yeast or crumble the compressed yeast over the water (110F if dry, 100F if compressed).  Add the pinch of sugar & allow yeast to sit in a draft-free spot for 10-20 minute. The mixture should be full of bubbles.  If not, the yeast is too old to be useful. Stir well to dissolve the yeast.  In a large bowl, place all the dry ingredients & stir until well blended.  Add the yeast mixture & 3 cups broth.  Using your hands, in the bowl, mix to form the dough, adding more broth if needed to make the dough smooth.  Half a batch at a time, knead the dough briefly on a lightly floured counter. (Keep the 2nd batch of dough covered with a moist towel while shaping and cutting the first)  Roll out the dough onto cookie sheet. Cut into your dog's favorite shapes.  Place on a greased baking sheet.  For a shiny finish, lightly beat together the egg and the milk. Brush the glaze on the cookies.  Bake at 300F for 45-60 minutes or until brown & firm.  Allow to cool completely and dry out until hard.

# *Buckwheat Dog Biscuits*

- ✔ 6 1/2 cups buckwheat flour
- ✔ 1 cup flax seed
- ✔ 1/2 cup nonfat powdered milk
- ✔ 2 cups fiber cereal
- ✔ 1 teaspoon salt
- ✔ 1 package dry yeast
- ✔ 1/4 cup warm water
- ✔ 2 cups low sodium tomato juice

# (Continued Buckwheat Dog Biscuits)

Combine all dry ingredients. Dissolve yeast in warm water and add tomato juice. Mix with dry ingredients. Dough should be very stiff. Knead dough for about 3 minutes. Roll out on floured board to 1/4 to 1/2 inch thickness. Cut into your dog's favorite shapes. Place on an un-greased cookie sheet and bake at 300F for 45 minutes. Allow to cool completely and dry out until hard.

# *Chicken flavored Dog Biscuits*

- ✔ 2 cups buckwheat flour

- ✔ 1/2 cup flax seed

- ✔ 1/2 cup yeast

- ✔ 3 tablespoons vegetable oil

- ✔ 1 cup chicken stock

Combine first 3 ingredients.  Mix well.  In a separate large mixing bowl, combine the stock and oil in a separate bowl.  Slowly stir flour mixture into oil and stock mixture until the dough is well-mixed.  Shape dough into a ball.  On lightly floured surface, roll out dough 1/2 inch thick.  Cut into your dog's favorite shapes.  Place on a greased baking sheet.  Bake at 400F for 20-25 minutes or until well-browned.  Allow to cool completely and dry out until hard.

# *Peanut Butter & Vanilla Biscuits*

- ✔ 1 1/2 cups water

- ✔ 1/2 cup oil

- ✔ 2 eggs

- ✔ 3 tablespoons organic gluten free peanut butter

- ✔ 2 teaspoons vanilla extracts (alcohol free)

- ✔ 2 cups buckwheat flour

- ✔ 1/2 cup flax seed meal

- ✔ 1/2 cup rice puffs

Blend wet ingredients together. Whisk dry ingredients together and mix into wet mixture to form a ball of dough. Roll out and cut into your dog's favorite shapes. Place onto greased cookie sheet. Bake at 400F for 20 minutes. Allow to cool completely and dry out until hard.

# *Tail Waggin' Biscuits*

- ✔ 1/3 cup margarine, softened

- ✔ 1/2 cup nonfat powdered milk

- ✔ 1 egg, beaten

- ✔ 3/4 cup hot water

- ✔ 3 cups buckwheat flour

In a large bowl pour hot water over margarine. Stir in powdered milk and egg. Add flour, 1/2 cup at a time until well blended. Knead 3 to 4 minutes, adding more flour if necessary to make very stiff dough. Roll to 1/2 inch thickness and cut into your dog's favorite shapes. Place on a greased cookie sheet and bake at 325F for 50 minutes. Allow to cool completely and dry out until hard.

# *Rice Noodle Treats*

- ✔ 1 cup crushed rice noodles

- ✔ 3/4 cup nonfat powdered milk

- ✔ 1/3 cup margarine

- ✔ 3/4 cup flax seed meal

- ✔ 1 bouillon cube

- ✔ 1 egg, beaten

- ✔ 1 1/2 cups hot water

- ✔ 3 cups buckwheat flour

In a large bowl pour hot water over oatmeal, margarine, and bouillon cube. Let stand 5 minutes. Stir in powdered milk, cornmeal and egg. Add flour, 1/2 cup at a time, until well blended. Knead 3-4 minutes, add more flour if necessary to stiffen dough. Pat or roll dough to 1/2 inch thickness. Cut into your dog's favorite shapes and place on a greased cookie sheet. Bake at 325F for 50 minutes. Allow to cool completely and dry out until hard.

# *Trail Dog Biscuits*

- ✔ 4 cups buckwheat flour

- ✔ 1 cup flax seed meal

- ✔ 1 3/4 cups chicken or beef broth

- ✔ 1/4 cup liver powder (available in health food stores)

- ✔ 1 egg, beaten

- ✔ 1 cup rice puffs

- ✔ 1/2 cup vegetable oil

Mix all dry ingredients in a large bowl. Add egg, oil, and beef broth. Mix the dough, add more flour if necessary to stiffen dough. On a floured surface, roll to 1/2 inch thickness, and then cut into your dog's favorite shapes. Place on a greased cookie sheet. Bake at 300F for 35-45 minutes. Allow to cool completely and dry out until hard.

# *Turkey & Cheese Treats*

- ✔ 2 cups turkey or chicken broth

- ✔ 4 cups cooked ground turkey or chicken

- ✔ 1 cup grated cheddar cheese

- ✔ 1 teaspoon poultry seasoning

- ✔ 2 cups crushed gluten free cracker crumbs

In a large bowl mix ground turkey, cheese, seasoning, 1 cup of crushed cracker crumbs and broth. Roll mixture into 1 inch balls. Roll balls into additional cracker crumbs. Place on an un-greased cookie sheet. Bake at 350F for 15-20 minutes or until cheese melts. Allow to cool completely and serve as desired.

# *Liver Treats*

- ✔ 1 pound beef liver

- ✔ 1 cup buckwheat flour

- ✔ 1 cup flax seed meal

- ✔ 2 eggs

Puree liver in food processor. Add eggs, whole buckwheat flour and flax seed meal. Pour onto greased cookie sheet. Bake at 350F for 25-30 minutes, flipping over halfway through baking. Cut into your dog's favorite shapes. Allow to cool completely and serve as desired.

# *Sweet Treats*

- ✔ 1 3/4 cups buckwheat flour

- ✔ 1/2 cup ground walnuts

- ✔ 1/4 cup sesame seeds

- ✔ 1 egg yolk

- ✔ 1/2 cup Splenda brown sugar

- ✔ 1/2 cup vanilla extracts (alcohol free)

- ✔ 12 tablespoons butter

- ✔ 4 tablespoons flax seed

- ✔ 1/2 cup water

Mix all ingredients in large bowl, knead until well blended. Roll out to 1/2 inch thick. Cut into your dog's favorite shapes. Place on an un-greased cookie sheet. Bake at 375F for 12-15 minutes. Allow to cool completely and serve as desired.

# *Bacon Bits*

- ✔ 6 slices cooked bacon, crumbled

- ✔ 4 eggs, well beaten

- ✔ 1/8 cup bacon fat

- ✔ 1 cup water

- ✔ 1/2 cup nonfat powdered milk

- ✔ 2 cup buckwheat flour

- ✔ 2 cup flax seed

- ✔ 1/2 cup flax seed meal

Mix all ingredients in a large bowl; drop heaping tablespoon onto a greased cookie sheet. Bake at 350F for 20-25 minutes. Allow to cool completely and dry out until hard.

# *Peanut Butter Treats*

- ✔ 1 1/2 cups buckwheat flour
- ✔ 1/4 cup organic gluten free peanut butter
- ✔ 1/2 cup water
- ✔ 1/4 cup vegetable oil or olive oil
- ✔ 3/4 cup rice puffs
- ✔ 1/4 cup flax seed
- ✔ 1/4 cup honey
- ✔ 1 cup brown rice flour
- ✔ 1/2 cup water

Mix all ingredients until well blended. Knead on floured surface until dough is stiff. Pat out to 1/4 inch thick. Cut into your dog's favorite shapes. Place on large un-greased cookie sheet. Bake at 350F for 25-35 minutes. Allow to cool completely and dry out until hard.

# *Tuna Treats*

- ✔ 1 cup flax seed meal

- ✔ 1 cup flax seed

- ✔ 1 small can tuna in oil (do not drain)

- ✔ 1/3 cup water

Grind flax seed meal in blender to make coarse flour. Set aside in small bowl. In food processor, whip tuna with the oil, and water then add remaining ingredients. Pulse until mixture forms a ball. Knead dough into a ball on floured surface. Roll out to a 1/4 inch thickness. Cut into your dog's favorite shapes. Place on lightly greased cookie sheet and bake at 350F for 25-35 minutes. Allow treats to cool complete and dry out until hard.

# *Dog Squares*

- ✔ 2 1/2 cups buckwheat flour

- ✔ 1/2 cup nonfat powdered milk

- ✔ 1 teaspoon Splenda brown sugar or honey

- ✔ 6 tablespoons of cold meat or bacon drippings

- ✔ 1 egg, slightly beaten

- ✔ 1/2 cup ice water

Mix flour, powdered milk and sugar. Fold in meat drippings until mixture has cornmeal texture. Mix in egg. Add enough water so that mixture forms a ball. Pat out dough to 1/2 inch thick. Cut into your dog's favorite shapes and place on a greased cookie sheet. Bake at 350F for 35-45 minutes. Allow to cool completely and dry out until hard.

# *Bad Breath Be-Gone*

- ✔ 2 cups brown rice flour

- ✔ 1 tablespoon activated charcoals (find this at pharmacies or health food stores, do not use charcoal briquettes)

- ✔ 3 tablespoons olive oil

- ✔ 1 egg

- ✔ 1/2 cup chopped fresh mint

- ✔ 1/2 cup chopped fresh parsley

- ✔ 2/3 cup nonfat powdered milk

- ✔ 1/2 cup chicken broth

Mix flour and charcoal until well blended then add other ingredients. Drop heaping teaspoon on a greased cookie sheet, about 1 inch apart. Bake at 400F for 25-30 minutes. Allow to cool completely and dry out until hard.

# *Training Snacks*

- ✔ 1/2 cup warm water
- ✔ 1/2 cup nonfat powdered milk
- ✔ 1 pound liver, chopped
- ✔ 1/2 cup toasted wheat germ
- ✔ 1 cup flax seed meal
- ✔ 1 cup buckwheat flour

Liquefy liver and water in food processor. Pour into a mixing bowl and add all other ingredients. Mix well to form a ball. Pat out to 1/2 inch thick. Cut into your dog's favorite shapes and place on greased cookie sheet. Bake at 350F for 30-40 minutes. Allow to cool completely and dry out until hard.

# *Peanut Bites*

- ✔ 1 cup buckwheat flour

- ✔ 3 tablespoons  organic gluten free peanut butter

- ✔ 1/4 cup hot water

- ✔ 1/8 cup chopped peanuts

- ✔ 1 tablespoon vegetable oil

- ✔ 1 egg, beaten

- ✔ 1 cup nonfat powdered milk

Mix all ingredients in bowl.  Add enough powdered milk to make firm dough.  Roll out dough to 1/2 inch thick.  Cut into your dog's favorite shapes and place on a greased cookie sheet.  Bake at 300F for 45 minutes. Allow to cool completely and dry out until hard.

# *Healthy Snacks*

- ✔ 1 3/4 cups buckwheat flour

- ✔ 2 teaspoons flax seed

- ✔ 1/2 cup Splenda brown sugar

- ✔ 1/4 cup sesame seeds

- ✔ 2 teaspoons margarine

- ✔ 1/2 cup ground walnuts

- ✔ 1/2 teaspoon vanilla extracts (alcohol free)
- ✔ 1/2 cup chicken broth

Mix all the ingredients. Knead until well blended. Pat out to 1/4 inch thick and cut into your dog's favorite shapes. Place on an un-greased cookie sheet. Bake at 375F for 25-30 minutes. Allow to cool completely and dry out until hard.

# *Veggie Vittles*

- ✔ 3 cups minced parsley
- ✔ 1/4 cup carrots, chopped very fine
- ✔ 1/4 cup shredded mozzarella or Parmesan cheese
- ✔ 2 tablespoons olive oil
- ✔ 3 cups buckwheat flour
- ✔ 2 tablespoons fiber cereal
- ✔ 1 cup of water

# (Continued Veggie Vittles)

Mix parsley, carrots, cheese, and oil in separate bowl. Mix remaining dry ingredients then combine mixtures. Gradually add 1/2 cup of water, mixing well. Make moist but not wet dough. Knead for one minute. Roll dough out to 1/2 inch thickness. Cut into your dog's favorite shapes and place on greased cookie sheet. Bake at 350F for 20-30 minutes, or until biscuits have browned and hardened slightly. Allow to cool completely and dry out until hard.

# *Yogurt Yummies*

- ✔ 32 oz gluten free, nonfat plain yogurt

- ✔ 3/4 cup water

- ✔ 1 chicken bouillon cube

Dissolve bouillon in water. Mix water and yogurt in blender until well blended. Pour into small plastic containers, cover with tin foil and freeze. Serve cold.

# *Peanut Pupcicles*

✔ 1 banana

✔ 1/2 cup organic gluten free peanut butter

✔ 1/4 cup flax seed

✔ 1/4 cup chopped peanuts

Mash bananas and peanut butter together, stir in flax seed and chopped peanuts. Chill 1 hour. With wet hands, place in container, store in refrigerator or freezer. Serve cold.

# *Doggy Chillers*

✔ 2 fresh beef or lamb marrow bones, each at least 1 inch long

✔ water

Place bones in a 2 quart pan; add enough water to cover the bones. Bring water to a boil; continue to boil for at least 10 minutes. Remove bones from broth. Pull off any beef marrow or meat from bones and chop into small bits then add to broth. Cool the broth to room temperature and pour into ice cube trays. Freeze and serve cold. Do not serve bones!

# *Puffed Up Pup Drops*

- ✔ 1/4 cup warm water

- ✔ 1 cup nonfat powdered milk

- ✔ 2 1/2 cups buckwheat flour

- ✔ 1/4 cup olive oil

- ✔ 1 egg

- ✔ 1 package sugar free unflavored gelatin

- ✔ 6 oz minced cooked chicken meat

- ✔ 1 package dry yeast

- ✔ 1/4 cup water

## (Continued Puffed Up Pup Drops)

Dissolve yeast in 1/4 cup warm water. Mix all dry ingredients together. Add the rest of the ingredients. Drop teaspoonful of dough onto a un-greased cookie sheet. Bake at 300F for 25 minutes. Allow to cool completely and dry until hard.

# *Pup Pleasers*

- ✔ 1/2 pound ground beef

- ✔ 1 carrot, finely grated

- ✔ 1 teaspoon grated cheese

- ✔ 1/2 cup gluten free cracker crumbs

- ✔ 1 egg, beaten

- ✔ 1 teaspoon tomato paste

Mix all ingredients until well blended. Roll into meat balls. Place on a greased cookie sheet. Bake at 350F for 25-30 minutes or until brown and firm. Allow to cool completely and store in refrigerator.

# *Canine Candy*

- ✔ 1/2 cup vegetable oil

- ✔ 1/2 cup shortening

- ✔ 1 cup honey

- ✔ 2 eggs

- ✔ 3 3/4 cups buckwheat flour

- ✔ 1/2 cup flax seed meal

- ✔ 2 teaspoons cinnamon

Mix vegetable oil, shortening, honey with eggs until well blended, add flour. Knead dough until mixed well. Roll dough into 1 inch balls. Mix the flax seed meal and cinnamon together in a bowl and roll balls in mixture. Place 2 inches apart on a greased cookie sheet. Press the balls down with a fork. Bake at 400F for 10-15 minutes. Allow to cool completely and serve as desired.

# *Wheat Free Salmon Surprise*

- ✔ 8 oz. can salmon with juice

- ✔ 1/2 cup chopped parsley

- ✔ 3 hard boiled eggs, shells included (shells are high in protein)

- ✔ 1/2 cup ground sesame seeds

- ✔ 1/2 cup flax seed meal

- ✔ 2-3 cups buckwheat flour

- ✔ 1/2 cup chicken broth

Mix all ingredients "except flour" into a food processor until well blended. Pour flour into mixture while processing. Roll dough out to 1/2 inch thickness. Cut into your dog's favorite shapes. Place on greased cookie sheets. Bake at 375F for 20-25 minutes. Turn and rotate the cookie sheets and bake about 10 more minutes. Allow to cool completely and dry out until hard.

# DOGGY DESSERT

# *Chicken Liver Cookies*

- ✔ 2 cups buckwheat flour

- ✔ 3 tablespoons vegetable oil

- ✔ 1 cup flax seed meal

- ✔ 1 egg, lightly beaten

- ✔ 1/2 cup chicken broth

- ✔ 2 teaspoons parsley

- ✔ 1 cup cooked chicken liver, chopped

Mix flour and flax seed meal In separate bowl, beat egg with oil, and then add broth and parsley until well blended. Add the dry ingredients to bowl a little at a time, stirring well. Fold in chicken livers and mix until dough is stiff. Knead dough on floured surface briefly. Roll out 1/2 inch thick and cut into your dog's favorite shapes. Place on greased cookie sheet 1 inch apart. Bake at 350F for 25-30 minutes or until firm. Allow to cool completely and dry out until hard.

# *Turkey Cookies*

- ✔ 3/4 cup butter or margarine

- ✔ 1/4 cup honey

- ✔ 2 cup buckwheat flour

- ✔ 2 cups flax seed

- ✔ 2 eggs

- ✔ 1 cup chopped "turkey" bacon

- ✔ 1 teaspoon vanilla extract (alcohol free)

- ✔ 2 cups coarsely crushed bran flake cereal

- ✔ 1/2 cup chicken broth

# (Continued Turkey Cookies)

In a large bowl, cream together the butter and honey. Beat in the eggs, chicken broth and vanilla extract. Add the flax seed and flour until well blended. Fold in the bacon. Gently fold in the cereal. Drop tablespoon onto greased cookie sheet. Bake at 350F for 20-25 minutes. Allow to cool completely and dry out until hard.

# *Jaxy's Favorite Dog Cookies*

✔ 2 cups buckwheat flour

✔ 1 cup vegetable oil

✔ 2/3 cup warm water

✔ 1/4 cup flax seed meal

✔ 1/4 teaspoon vanilla or mint flavoring (alcohol free)

Mix all ingredients in large bowl until well blended. Roll out to 1/4 inch thick. Cut into your dog's favorite shapes. Place on lightly greased cookie sheet. Bake at 350F for 30 minutes. Allow to cool completely and dry out until hard.

# *Soft Chews*

- ✔ 3 (2 1/2 oz. each) jars of baby food; either beef or chicken

- ✔ 1/4 cup nonfat powdered milk

- ✔ 1/4 cup buckwheat meal

Mix all ingredients in large bowl until well blended. Roll into small balls and place on greased cookie sheet. Flatten slightly with a fork. Bake at 350F for 15-25 minutes or until brown. Allow to cool completely and store in refrigerator.

# *Doggy Ice Cream*

- ✔ 32 oz. gluten free plain yogurt

- ✔ 1 mashed banana

- ✔ 2 tablespoons organic gluten free peanut butter

- ✔ 2 tablespoons honey

Mix all ingredients together and freeze in either 3 ounce paper cups or ice cube trays. Allow to thaw slightly before serving.

# *Banana Biscotti*

- ✔ 5 cups buckwheat flour
- ✔ 1/4 cup vegetable oil
- ✔ 1/4 cup chopped peanuts
- ✔ 1 1/2 cups bananas pureed
- ✔ 1 egg
- ✔ 2 teaspoons vanilla extract (alcohol free)
- ✔ water

# (Continued Banana Biscotti)

Mix dry ingredients in a large bowl. Make a well in the center. Blend egg, oil and banana. Add dry ingredients into the well. Add water, one teaspoon at a time as needed. Knead by hand until well blended. Form into logs approximately 2-2 1/2 inches high. Flatten so that log is 6-7 inches wide by 1 inch high. Place on lightly greased cookie sheet. Bake at 325F for 30-40 minutes. Allow to cool for 10 minutes. Slice into 1/2 inch slices. Place on cookie sheet and bake for another 20 minutes or until golden brown. Allow to cool completely and serve as desired.

# *Carob Cake*

- ✔ 1 1/2 cups buckwheat flour

- ✔ 1/2 cup nonfat powdered milk

- ✔ 1/4 cup of margarine softened

- ✔ 4 egg yolks

- ✔ 1 teaspoon vanilla extract (alcohol free)

- ✔ 1/2 teaspoon salt

- ✔ 2 ounces of melted carob

- ✔ 1 cup water

- ✔ 1 16 oz gluten free plain yogurt

Grease and flour loaf pan, 9x5x3. Mix all ingredients in a large bowl. Pour into loaf pan. Bake at 350F For 45 minutes. Allow to cool completely. Frost with gluten free plain yogurt. Serve as desired.

# *Pet Party Cake*

- ✔ 1 1/2 cups buckwheat flour

- ✔ 1 jar beef or liver baby food (2 1/2-ounce)

- ✔ 1/2 cup margarine, softened

- ✔ 4 eggs

- ✔ 1/2 cup olive oil

- ✔ 3 strips dog beef jerky, crumbled

- ✔ gluten free plain yogurt for icing

# (Continued Pet Party Cake)

In large bowl, with electric mixer at medium speed, cream margarine until smooth. Add corn oil, baby food and eggs; mix until smooth. At low speed, gradually beat flour mixture into beef mixture until batter is smooth. Fold in beef jerky. Pour batter into well-greased and floured 8x5x3 loaf pan. Bake at 325F for 45 minutes to an hour. Remove from pan to cool completely. Cut into 1/2 inch slices. Ice each slice with yogurt.

# *Apple Ruffin' Muffin*

✔ 2 3/4 cups water

✔ 1 cup dried apple chips (no seeds)

✔ 1/4 cup applesauce, unsweetened

✔ 1 egg, beaten slightly

✔ 1/4 teaspoon vanilla extract (alcohol free)

✔ 4 tablespoons honey

✔ 4 cups buckwheat flour

Spray muffin tin with pan spray. Mix all wet ingredients thoroughly. Mix dry ingredients in separate bowl. Add wet ingredients to dry ingredients until well blended. Pour into muffin tins. Bake at 350F for 45 minutes. Allow to cool completely and serve as desired.

# *Best Friend Bread Pudding*

- ✔ 2 cups scalded milk (just before boiling point)

- ✔ 1/2 cup Splenda

- ✔ 1/2 teaspoon salt

- ✔ 1/2 teaspoon vanilla extract (alcohol free)

- ✔ 8 eggs

- ✔ 5 slices gluten free bread

Grease baking dish with butter or margarine. Cube 5 slices of bread and put in baking dish. In a bowl, mix 8 eggs, 1/2 cup sugar, 1/2 teaspoon salt and 1/2 teaspoon vanilla. Add 2 cups scalded milk and beat with wire whisk. Pour mixture into baking dish on top of cubed bread. Place baking dish in pan of water and bake at 325F for 45 minutes. Allow to cool completely and serve as desired. Store in refrigerator.

# *Canine Corn Bread*

✔ 1 cup flax seed meal

✔ 1 cup buckwheat flour

✔ 1 cup milk

✔ 1 egg, beaten

✔ 1/2 cup bacon grease or olive oil

Mix all dry ingredients in separate large bowl. Add wet ingredients and beat until smooth. Pour into a greased, 8 inch square baking pan. Bake at 425F for 15-20 minutes. Allow to cool completely and serve as desired. Store in refrigerator.

# *Roll-Over-Rolls*

### *Light Dough*

- ✔ 4 cups buckwheat flour
- ✔ 1/2 cup flax seed meal
- ✔ 1 egg
- ✔ 1/4 cup organic, gluten free peanut butter
- ✔ 1 1/2 cups water

### *Dark Dough*

- ✔ 4 cups buckwheat flour
- ✔ 1/2 cup flax seed meal
- ✔ 1 egg
- ✔ 1/4 cup molasses
- ✔ 1/2 teaspoon cinnamon
- ✔ 1 tablespoon canola oil
- ✔ 1 1/2 cups water

# (continued Roll-Over-Rolls)

Mix each color dough ingredients separately. Knead each color, adding flour as necessary to stiffen dough. Roll light dough on floured surface into a 1/2-inch thick rectangle. Roll the dark dough to the same dimensions. Damp the top of the light dough with water, then lay dark dough on top. Roll tightly from the long edge like a jellyroll. Wrap in plastic wrap and freeze for 1 hour. Cut 1/2inch thick slices and place on greased cookie sheet. Bake at 350F for 1 hour. Allow to cool completely and dry out to hard.

# *Index*

# Create your own recipe

# Create your own recipe

# Create your own recipe

19489549R00056

Made in the USA
Lexington, KY
20 December 2012